IMAGES
of America

KNIGHTSVILLE
AND SILVER LAKE

IMAGES
of America

KNIGHTSVILLE
AND SILVER LAKE

Joe Fuoco and A.J. Lothrop

ARCADIA
PUBLISHING

Copyright © 1998 by Joe Fuoco and A.J. Lothrop
ISBN 978-0-7385-6435-7

Published by Arcadia Publishing
Charleston SC, Chicago IL, Portsmouth NH, San Francisco CA

Printed in the United States of America

Library of Congress Catalog Card Number: 2009920449

For all general information contact Arcadia Publishing at:
Telephone 843-853-2070
Fax 843-853-0044
E-mail sales@arcadiapublishing.com
For customer service and orders:
Toll-Free 1-888-313-2665

Visit us on the Internet at www.arcadiapublishing.com

*This book is for those who settled
the villages of Knightsville and Silver Lake;
for the courageous, intrepid voyagers of over 100 years ago,
who sought a new life in a new world,
while preserving the values of the old.*

Contents

Acknowledgments

Gratitude is extended to those who so generously contributed to this book. I want to thank St. Bartholomew Church, St. Mary's Church, St. Ann's Church, Mr. and Mrs. Robert Kennedy, Al Lothrop, the family of Josephine De Rotto, the Sprague Mansion, the St. Mary Society, and all the others who took the time to collect old photographs.

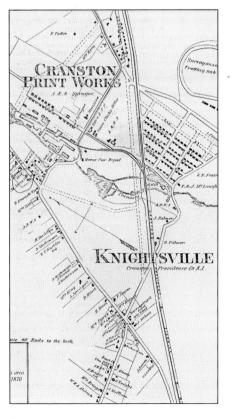

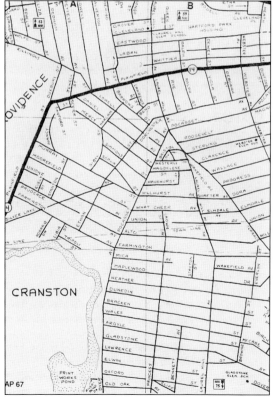

Introduction

They are sister villages—each unique, yet connected not only by physical proximity but in a very real sense by the flow of a river, the Pocasset, that runs through them; by some pieces of infamous history, for both were the settings of lurid murders; and by a quality of the old, still preserved through change.

Today, Knightsville is in Cranston, and Silver Lake is a part of Providence, but one may easily walk the short distance that connects these old, historic villages. Though similar in the way they were settled, the two villages have their own ethos: Knightsville is more compact, more central, while Silver Lake is spread, expansive. And each has its own history.

One day in the year 1843, industrialist Amasa Sprague of the famous Spragues, owners of many mills and the holders of important political offices, took a walk. He strolled from his mansion across what is now the St. Ann Cemetery, a sprawling Roman Catholic cemetery with elegant stones and monuments and lofty gates, where an ancient slate-marked corner contains the remains of the Dyers and other English families. Amasa was on his way across the fields when he was shot and killed. In those days, the hatred between the English settlers and the Irish was profound. An Irishman, John Gordon, was charged with the murder, found guilty, and executed, hanged in Providence at the foot of the present state capital building. His was the last execution ever performed in the state of Rhode Island, for it was determined later that John Gordon very likely did not kill Amasa Sprague, but was blamed because of the anti-Irish bias that permeated the state. Thus emerged one of the legendary events in the history of an area called Knightsville, Cranston, an event that changed the penal system in Rhode Island forever.

Knightsville was once called Monkeytown. The reason for the name is lost. It is recorded nowhere but on old maps hanging in the city hall of Cranston. For years, beginning in the 1880s, Knightsville was the seat of government for Cranston; its town clerk's office gave way to a new town house in 1866. But even long before, town meetings were held in Nehemiah Knight's tavern on the site of the present city building. In 1754, the first town council was organized in Caleb Arnold's tavern, and for half a century town meetings were held in the old Knightsville meetinghouse, still standing.

A village of mill houses, old factories, small streets, a large cemetery, and a wonderful square, Knightsville is really one of the last remaining areas of immigrant settlement. In its early days it was known for the selling of liquor, and its old buildings, with wide doorways and the remains of ancient bars, are testimony to that. Settled first by the English, its name is a tribute to the Knight family, to the aforementioned Nehemiah Knight, an innkeeper, town clerk, representative in Congress (from 1817 to 1821), and U.S. senator (from 1821 to 1841). Some of its streets and great houses bear the names of those hardy English emigres and entrepreneurs, streets like Dyer

Avenue, the Sprague Mansion, and the former Sprague Print Works (later called the Cranston Print Works).

In the early 1900s Knightsville overflowed with Italian immigrants, largely from a village called Itri, a small town between Rome and Naples. These immigrants, descendants of whom still live in the village, stamped their unique ethos upon the village. They erected their churches, literally stone by stone, worked as farmers, bricklayers, and masons, and virtually built Knightsville into a thriving industrial community. Small streets are still dotted with echoes of little stores, shops, and small businesses.

To say that Knightsville became an Italian community is to emphasize the solidity of the Italian people who came to the village. The Itri of Italy is often called the sister city of the Itrani, people of Itri who settled in Knightsville. To this day, festivals in Italy's Itri are coordinated with the same religious festivals in Knightsville, the patron saint being Maria Di Civita. So close is this association that filmmaker Salvatore Mancini has made a film called *The Americanization of Itri*, which beautifully dramatizes this melding of cultures.

In 1921, the Italian population in Knightsville had reached almost 4,000. As an immigrant people, they considered their treatment by Bishop William A. Hickey a persecution. A committee was formed called the Italian Committee of Cranston, stating that "the Italian people are ready to make any sacrifice, provided they are delivered from their present slavery and continuous persecutions of the American priest against all Italians." The Bishop was pressured into creating St. Mary's Parish for the Italian community. Today, a church like St. Mary's alone has a congregation of 14,000.

Knightsville is largely intact. The square is still a center of community gatherings, the churches at the cemetery gates are still vital in the lives of the people, and the mills remain standing along with the Sprague Mansion and the streets of row houses. It is an old neighborhood altered but not made extinct by the incursions of the new. Knightsville, the village, is still an example of New England Americana, now ethnically diverse, but still connected to its history.

There is no Silver Lake! Of course, by that I mean that no lake called Silver any longer exists. Once, there was a large water-filled basin, used for amusements in the late 1800s and early 1900s, but the lake was finally dredged, and the basin filled in. Today, streets and tenements and private homes occupy the site, along with a market and a number of businesses, car lots, vegetable and fruit stands, a baseball park, a neighborhood pool, and the mighty hill down which sledders still speed called Neutokonkanut Hill.

Silver Lake, which is sometimes defined as an area between Laurel Hill Avenue and Neutokonkanut Hill, is rich in history. In 1902 it was no longer a part of the town of Johnston but the West Side of Providence. In a few years, the great wave of immigrants had established their own church in the Lake, as it is still known today. An area rich in immigrant ethos, its streets still revere the names of old English settlers buried as far back as the late 1700s in the Pocasset Cemetery, a treasure trove of historical data. Here the Watermans, the Fenners, the Dyers, and the Tripps are buried along streets called Maple Avenue, Park Avenue, and Oak Bluff Avenue.

Religion looms very large in Silver Lake, and it is impossible to speak of the Lake without considering the important part its churches have played in keeping the neighborhood relatively intact. Today, despite changing demographics, the narrow streets and converted mansions of another era remain, as do the remnants of old churches, sprawling abandoned estates, clubs, and what remains of a square. Its main street, Pocasset Avenue, joins Dyer Avenue, thus creating an uninterrupted stretch of road from the Lake to Knightsville. A hot bed of political campaigning, Silver Lake for generations has been a seething, sometimes explosive, pocket of political warfare. To this day, it is perceived throughout Rhode Island as one of the areas most saturated by political signs, posters, banners, et al during any given election year. It was also the setting, years ago, of its own murder, even rivaling that of Amasa Sprague in Knightsville. It has managed to retain its village look, and thousands of descendants of turn-of-the-century immigrants still live here.

One

Origins:
Places in the Heart

A welcome to the historic place called Silver Lake, of which no lake any longer exists. Compact, not as sprawling as other villages, Silver Lake still encompasses a large area.

A dramatic view of Itri showing the ruins of its majestic castle lording over the typical Italian village houses. Notice the tile roofs of these ancient structures. (Photograph courtesy of St. Mary Feast Society.)

The walled city of Itri with its striking castle. Sweeping up the side of a mountain, the town was a vulnerable place during World War II. From here came the Itrani, who settled in Knightsville, keeping a connection to their European origin vitally alive. (Photograph courtesy of the St. Mary Feast Society.)

A view of the town of Itri showing the Castello (Castle) with some of its walls still standing. (Photograph courtesy of St. Mary Feast Society.)

Itri Square, located in the very center of the village of Knightsville. In the circle of stone is a map of the old village, the sister village in Italy called Itri.

The Virgin of Itri in the very familiar pose. This image is unmistakable, the seated Virgin with the Christ Child in her lap. Saint Mary's Feast Society keeps the old fires burning.

A feast and festival moving along the small roads leading from the village in the distance. Throngs such as this were ordinary for festivals. Notice the flag held by the child in the wagon, and the painting of La Madonna Di Civita, the all important saint of veneration, Itri's holy virgin. (Photograph courtesy of St. Mary Feast Society.)

The devastation of war. Bombs that were dropped on Monte Casino also destroyed much of Itri. The people suffered much during World War II.

Many citizens of Silver Lake pose for a lofty camera shot on Plainfield Street.

World War II refugees of Itri in 1944, before the end of the conflict. Reduced to virtually nothing, becoming but numbers in the vast arena of casualties, they had the friendship of Mussolini and Hitler to thank for this.

A destroyed church in Itri, in a photograph from 1944, illustrating the random destruction experienced by the village.

The Monte Civita Band. Ninety percent of the men in this remarkable photograph are immigrants. The photograph was taken on the steps of the Dean Mansion (located in the affluent Dean Estates). This band competed with the Victor Emanuelle III Band. (Photograph courtesy of St. Mary Feast Society.)

An aerial shot of a portion of Silver Lake, with the Church of St. Bartholomew at the center. Unlike the immigrants of Knightsville, most of whom emigrated from Itri, the Italian settlers of Silver Lake came from a number of villages, including Caserta, Frosinone, Benevento, and Napoli. (Photograph courtesy of St. Bartholomew Church.)

A bucolic scene photographed in Benevento, one of the places from which settlers of Silver Lake emigrated. An ancient city, Benevento is also the place of legends; the Seven Witches of Benevento (Le Sette Streghe Di Benevento) is one of the most famous ones. (Photograph by Esther Bubley.)

One of the crowded, jam-packed, laundry-shaded streets of Naples. From Naples came many of the settlers of Silver Lake. From Naples also came the unequaled Sophia Loren! (Photograph by Karl Gullers.)

Two

The Workplace

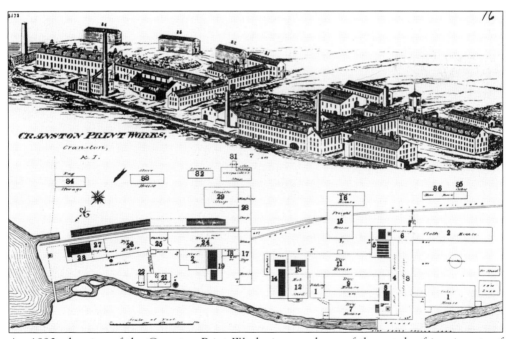

An 1890s drawing of the Cranston Print Works, an employer of thousands of immigrants of Silver Lake and Knightsville. Originally called the Sprague Mill, it was built and owned by one of the most famous of Rhode Island families.

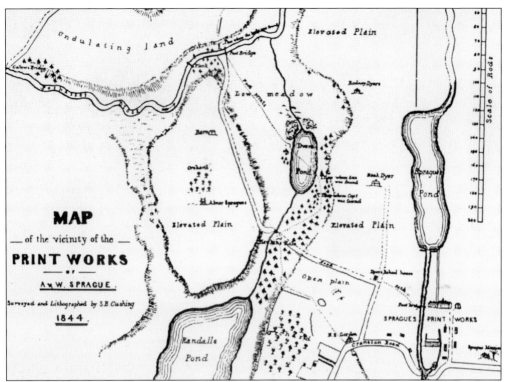

A map of the print works and its vicinity from an 1844 rendering. The Pocasset Brook (now called the Pocasset River) still meanders, serpentine-like; the open plain is now St. Anne's Cemetery.

Workers at the turn of the century on Budlong Farm, Pontiac Avenue. This photograph, taken around 1900, illustrates the back-breaking labor women who worked in the fields undertook. Notice the overseer with his chart. Men still did the ordering.

A very historic photograph of the Cranston Print Works in its infancy. Large as it was, it would grow enormously, feeding the immigrants, providing them with lodgings (mill or row houses) and enough coal to keep them reasonably warm during New England winters. The row houses to the far right are still occupied.

The Print Works today. Notice the tower, which still stands precisely as it did in the 1800s. Its lofty window has been sealed over, however. It was in these buildings the Irish replaced Yankee workers, only to be replaced themselves by immigrants from Italy.

Another view of the Print Works. The old architectural style of the New England mill has been preserved, and the whole structure is on the Historic Register. The sprawling complex was the first mill to manufacture hand-printed calico cloth in the United States.

The "new" front to the old mill, the corporate headquarters of the Cranston Print Works. This building was a testament to the illustrious Spragues—William became a congressman, governor, and senator, and his sons, Amasa and William, became two of the richest and most powerful men in Rhode Island. It was said that Amasa ran the mills . . . and all of Cranston!

A beautiful view of the Print Works and its river. The view was undoubtedly not so lovely for the Irish mill workers, who worked 13 to 16 hours a day and were treated with little mercy.

Row houses, many of which look today exactly as they did nearly 200 years ago. Take away the cars and the telephone poles, and you have a street out of the history of immigrant labor. This area is really the bridge between Knightsville (in the foreground) and Silver Lake (in the distance).

A fence offers an unusual, almost prison-like aspect to the Print Works. It is an evocation of another kind of bondage, that of the immigrant worker to the long hours and meager pay, subservient to an authority that despised them.

A Silver Lake baker with a magnificent load of bread. The big street of "the Lake," Pocasset Avenue has been known for decades for its breads and pastries. Ann's Bakery was a staple of the avenue for many years, but is now gone.

The Romano Funeral Home, located on a pivotal corner in Silver Lake. Father and sons and grandsons still operate this very well-known funeral parlor. The marble plaque is resonant of ancient Rome. Thousands of Silver Lake residents have come and gone at Romano's over the decades.

The original Nardolillo Funeral Home, a historic building dating to before 1907 on Pocasset Avenue. The Nardolillo Funeral Home, one of the most renowned in Rhode Island, has been a family operation for nearly 90 years.

The Nardolillo Funeral Home today—big, imposing, and moving into the twenty-first century. Beginning in what is Silver Lake, it is now located on Park Avenue on the very edge of Knightsville, thus spanning the two historic villages.

Two staples of the Italian diet—sausage and wine. For many Italians, life is not possible without these, nor should it be. The Silver Lake sausage shop has occupied this corner for decades, and customers, possibly since Prohibition ended, have been coming to the building next door for their wine-making supplies. Cheers! Or more appropriately, Salut!

One of the old images of Silver Lake, the corner gas station. Notice the flying pegasus, the logo of Richlube. Several families have owned this station, notably the Gelfuso brothers of the 1940s and 1950s. The building is now a memory. (Photograph courtesy of Mr. and Mrs. Robert Kennedy.)

A window display of the Pullano and Sons Market decorated for Christmas in the 1930s. Again, neatness and symmetry are the hallmarks of this well-remembered neighborhood market.

Pullano's and Sons Market in Silver Lake. Those who could, who had the talent, the trade, and the opportunity, not to mention the sheer courage, opened up their own businesses. Note the stocked shelves! To the left are the words, "Good Friday, April 7, 1939." Notice the absolute cleanliness and neatness of this village market.

The operators of Pullano's Market in 1936. From left to right are Elmo Pullano, Nicholas Pullano, John Geremia, Mr. Scungio, young Louis J. Pullano, and Luigi Pullano.

Three

A Murder in Knightsville

The famed Sprague Mansion. It was from here that Amasa Sprague, a rich and powerful member of the Sprague family, walked on December 31, 1843—the day he was murdered. The old section of the mansion is shrouded by the full trees of late summer.

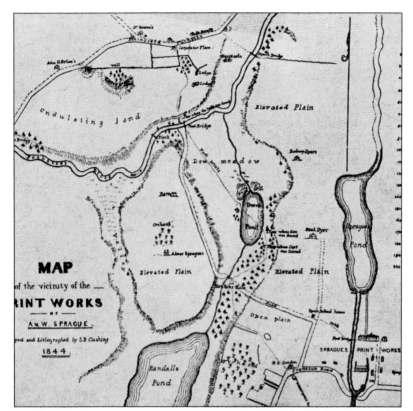

A map used at the trial of Irishman John Gordon, who was accused, with his brothers Nicholas and William, of the murder of Amasa. In the lower right-hand corner, notice the proximity of the Gordons' house to the Sprague Mansion. Today the Gordons' house and store are where the front walk of St. Ann's Church is located. (Map courtesy of St. Ann's Church.)

An exit to oblivion? Perhaps the unfortunate Amasa came out of the house via this side door and walked about the front of the mansion on his way to Thornton where, according to reports, he was going to check his farm, or was going on a very personal assignation that has never been fully revealed.

Amasa Sprague. Amasa was a noted bigot and hater of Irish immigrants, and he taunted Nicholas Gordon with racial epithets.

A contemporary sketch of the murder. The whole family of Gordons was arrested—even their mother, their 12-year-old sister, and the family dog!

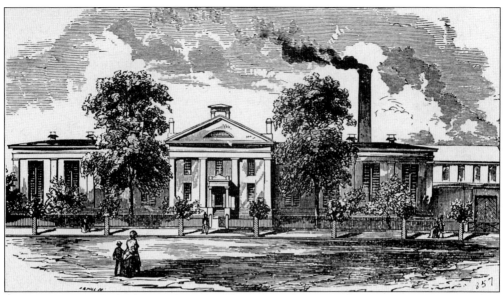

The tiny prison cell of John Gordon. It was here that John languished for more than a year. His brothers were set free—William was acquitted and Nicholas was never brought to trial—but John, in a virulent anti-Catholic atmosphere wherein the judge, Job Durfee, even instructed the jury to "distinguish" between the testimony of foreigners (Irish Catholics) and people of New England, was found guilty and hanged, protesting his innocence. On the scaffold, Fr. John Brady, standing next to Gordon, said, "You are going to join the noble band of martyrs of your countrymen, who have suffered before at the shrine of bigotry and prejudice."

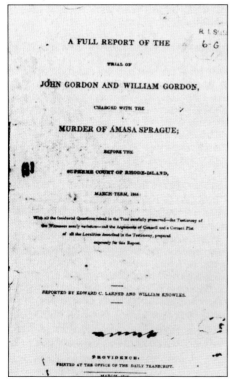

The 1844 court report of the Gordon murder trial, brought before the Supreme Court of Rhode Island. So unjust was this trial and execution, it precipitated the abolishment of capital punishment in Rhode Island seven years later, and that has stood until today. (Photograph courtesy of St. Ann's Church.)

The interior of the living room of the old section of the Sprague Mansion. Beautiful, not luxurious, but stately, Amasa must have spent much time here in the evenings, sitting before a blazing fire, never anticipating what would occur on the fateful night in 1843.

The tombstone of Amasa Sprague, enshrined in the Sprague Mansion. It states that Amasa was born in Cranston and murdered in Johnston on December 31, 1843, in his 40th year.

The site of the prison that held John Gordon. Where the accused awaited his execution, now a great mall is rising. To the right of the building under demolition (Rhode Island College) is where the prison stood. Recently, its ruined foundations were unearthed. This is where John Gordon languished for more than a year, waiting to be hanged a few yards away for the murder of Amasa Sprague. The site was the scene of the last execution in Rhode Island.

Four

The Churches

St. Bartholomew Church in Silver Lake, the way it looked after its enlargement in the 1920s to accommodate its growing parish. In 18 years the congregation had multiplied considerably. (Photograph courtesy of St. Bartholomew Church.)

The first St. Bartholomew Church in Silver Lake. Dedicated on September 22, 1907, it was considered too large for its congregation. Eighteen years later, it was much too small. Reverend Leonardo Quaglia was its first pastor; he remained pastor for six years. (Photograph courtesy of St. Bartholomew Church.)

The first nursery staffed by the Scalabrinian fathers called the Scalabrini Day Nursery and St. Bartholomew's Hall in Silver Lake. (Photograph courtesy of St. Bartholomew Church.)

The enlarged interior of the old St. Bartholomew Church. Ornate, reflecting churches of its type in southern Italy, it is a style long vanished, and is today considered archaic. (Photograph courtesy of St. Bartholomew Church.)

The lower church. The upper church itself was soon insufficient. Notice the use of life-size and larger-than-life-size statues of saints, a practice virtually abandoned in today's churches. (Photograph courtesy of St. Bartholomew Church.)

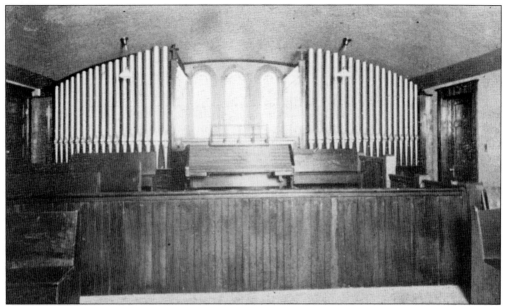

The new organ, located in the choir loft of the enlarged church of St. Bartholomew in the 1920s. A superb instrument for its time, its choir loft accommodated many singers. The present church, in the style of churches of the 1960s, has placed its smaller organ on the floor near the main altar. But the tradition of big, three-keyboard organs in choir lofts is returning. (Photograph courtesy of St. Bartholomew Church.)

The convent and the parish hall. Both have since been sold, and are shown here in their prime over 50 years ago. St. Bartholomew Church has in its relocation to its present lofty edifice retained virtually nothing of its holdings in the area of the older church. (Photograph courtesy of St. Bartholomew Church.)

The first enrollment of St. Bartholomew's School. Staffed by the Pallotine Sisters, the school dates from the 1950s. (Photograph courtesy of St. Bartholomew Church.)

Pallotine nuns in a 50-year-old photograph. This was the faculty of St. Bartholomew's School at the time. The manner of dress has since passed into history. The times have changed many things. (Photograph courtesy of St. Bartholomew Church.)

The St. Bartholomew Parochial School body. A great number of students are represented. The school is renowned for its excellence, and its students through the years have entered the finest high schools and colleges in the country. (Photograph courtesy of St. Bartholomew Church.)

Schoolchildren of St. Bartholomew's Parochial School. The children seem absolutely riveted by a charismatic teacher . . . or they know they are being photographed and are on their best behavior. (Photograph courtesy of St. Bartholomew Church.)

A controlled assembly of students in the schoolyard of St. Bartholomew's Parochial School. Notice the strategic positions of the nuns and the priest. (Photograph courtesy of St. Bartholomew Church.)

St. Bartholomew's Day Nursery 50 years ago. A thriving community of students and younger children, St. Bartholomew pioneered in the area of Silver Lake. That *all* kids should be so relaxed and at ease at 12:50 p.m.! (Photograph courtesy of St. Bartholomew Church.)

The Mother's Club. Where there are kids there are mothers. This smiling, happy group sits in the cafetorium of the St. Bartholomew School, flanked by nuns. (Photograph courtesy of St. Bartholomew Church.)

Confirmation in the old St. Bartholomew Church. The ornate ambience of the scene evokes a way of ceremonial many today consider old fashioned, but its echo of the old custom is irresistible in the historic sense. (Photograph courtesy of St. Bartholomew Church.)

Children are blessed at the altar railing of St. Bartholomew Church. This scene might be out of any neo-realistic Italian movie of the 1940s and '50s. All that is needed is an Anna Magnani or a Vittorio De Sica. (Photograph courtesy of St. Bartholomew Church.)

One of the many societies of St. Bartholomew Church that once flourished. This is the Italian Holy Name Society, no longer in existence, superceded by the Holy Name Society.

The English Holy Name Society. Both societies are now included in the Holy Name Society of the church. Today St. Bartholomew's, as with many parishes, has become so demographically diverse there is no politically correct way to address the situation but to include all in a single name. (Photograph courtesy of St. Bartholomew Church.)

Another church organization, known as the Third Order.

The Third Order. The group, which no longer exists, is shown here preparing for its annual retreat. (Photograph courtesy of St. Bartholomew Church.)

The daughters of Isabella of St. Bartholomew Church. This active group is still very much alive, arranging many activities such as the May crowning of the Virgin each year. (Photograph courtesy of St. Bartholomew Church.)

The St. Bartholomew's Mothers Guild. An extremely vital and active group, it has lasted through the years, and is today known as the St. Bartholomew Guild. (Photograph courtesy of St. Bartholomew Church.)

A sermon being given by Monsignor John L. Drury in the old St. Bartholomew Church. The occasion was the opening ceremony of the building campaign to build the new church. (Photograph courtesy of St. Bartholomew Church.)

John O. Pastore (center) and St. Bartholomew parishioners. John O. Pastore, a former governor of Rhode Island and U.S. senator, was a vibrant, articulate man who once addressed the Democratic National Convention with the fire and passion of a TV evangelist! He is surrounded here by parishioners at the ground-breaking ceremonies for the St. Bartholomew Parochial School. (Photograph courtesy of St. Bartholomew Church.)

The Most Rev. Russel J. McVinney D.D. of Providence.Rev. McVinney is blessing the recently completed St. Bartholomew School in Silver Lake. The dedication took place on August 23, 1953. (Photograph courtesy of St. Bartholomew Church.)

The former St. Bartholomew Youth Center, later sold with several nearby church properties.

The facade of the very contemporary St. Bartholomew Rectory, located very close to the new church. The state-of-the-art rectory was dedicated on April 13, 1969, replacing a stately three-story wooden structure which has since been razed.

Father Joseph Pranzo, C.S. Pastor, in front of the present St. Bartholomew Church, which was built in 1967. Located on top of a hill on Laurel Hill Avenue, it occupies a dramatic spot, and its tower can be seen from afar.

La proprieta'della Chiesa (meaning simply "church property") at No. 598 Union Avenue. This area was purchased in the very early years of immigrant settlement by St. Bartholomew Church. (Photograph courtesy of Mr. and Mrs. Robert Kennedy.)

The Campana of Silver Lake. The bell summoned parishioners to church, and was first placed in its bell tower in 1926, in the enlarged church. Affectionately called the Bell of Silver Lake, it was a survivor and a symbol to all who answered to its ring. (Photograph courtesy of Mr. and Mrs. Robert Kennedy.)

Another elegant, stately property of the church on Laurel Hill Avenue. Years later this area would become the core of the present church and its school. (Photograph courtesy of Mr. and Mrs. Robert Kennedy.)

The altar of the Madonna del Rosario in the old St. Bartholomew Church. Such shrines are now memories, for although shrines are implemented in the construction of contemporary churches, they are quite different in design from this decidedly Italianate style. (Photograph courtesy of Mr. and Mrs. Robert Kennedy.)

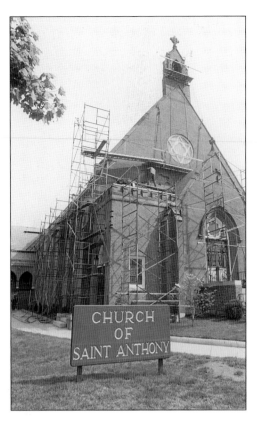

The Church of St. Anthony under renovation. Once one of the largest parishes, its congregation consisting largely of Irish immigrants and their descendants, the church today is greatly reduced in numbers; its once well-occupied large rectory is now the abode of a single priest; its convent has been sold; and its parochial school has been leased.

What is left of the old St. Bartholomew Church. The bell tower, preserved and maintained by the City of Providence, is still the site of various ceremonies and pilgrimages from the new church on the hill. About it is a lovely park. The wonderful bell remains.

Another view of the St. Anthony Church, a red brick edifice on Plainfield Street. Once a large choir sang in the loft of this church, but it, too, has been greatly reduced. Still, many of the area faithful are devoted to this church, and are loathe to leave.

The large, beautiful rectory of St. Anthony Church. Though it is hard to believe, this magnificent home for priests is the abode of a single shepherd to his flock. Behind may be seen a glimpse of the former parochial school, now a controversial center for psychological treatment of the young.

The superb stone structure that served as St. Anthony's convent for decades. Sold to the City of Providence, it is now the Silver Lake Senior Center, and has no affiliation with the church. Still, if one looks closely at its windows, it is not hard to "see" the nuns of many years ago sitting at those windows.

The shrine of Our Lady of Fatima next to St Anthony's Rectory. It is not uncommon to pass on Plainfield Street and see parishioners and believers standing and kneeling before this enclosed shrine.

The corner where the old church of St Bartholomew stood. The spot is virtually a venerated site, where feasts such as that of Corpus Christi are celebrated with prayer and hymns.

Statues of two of the three children who claimed to see the Virgin in Portugal in the early part of this century. A popular shrine, it attracts people in every season.

The new church of St. Bartholomew. To the right, in the corner, notice the half-torso statue of St. Bartholomew, rescued and restored from the old church, and placed for veneration on a new pedestal.

St Mary's Church in Knightsville, sister church to St. Ann's (a few hundred feet to its right). Both of these churches flank St. Ann's Cemetery. St. Mary's, better known as the church of Madonna Di Civita, the patron saint of Itri, is a magnificent edifice, imposing and dramatic in an Italian way.

St. Mary's Rectory. This large, elegant, superbly-landscaped building is the residence of the several priests who staff the church, which was once the largest Roman Catholic church in Cranston, and possibly the state.

The shrine room of Santa Maria Di Civita, patron Saint of the Itrani, located in St. Mary's Feast building in Knightsville. This is as much a social gathering place as anything else.

A general view of the sister church of Santa Maria Di Civita, in Itri, Italy. A procession winds down the mountain and through the streets of the village. In Knightsville, take away the mountain, and you still have the same kind of veneration and procession. (Photograph courtesy of St. Mary's Church.)

Carrying the statue of the seated Santa Maria Di Civita through the streets from the old St. Rocco's Church. This is a very early photograph of a feast at the turn of the century. Notice the trellis of flowers decorating the statue. The immigrants of Itri used St. Rocco's Church for the feast since at the time they did not have their own church. (Photograph courtesy of St. Mary's Church.)

A modern version of St. Mary's Feast, this one emanating from St. Mary's Church in Knightsville. The seated statue is unchanged in its traditional look. (Photograph courtesy of St. Mary's Church.)

Father Cesare Schettini, pastor of St. Mary's Church, with a ground-breaking shovel. The date is Palm Sunday, April 14, 1935. Before that time, the parishioners attended the old St. Rocco's Church, awaiting their own to be built. (Photograph courtesy of St. Mary's Church.)

St. Ann's Church, the first church, as it looked in 1858. This church, facing St. Mary's in Knightsville, was the so-called "Irish Church" as opposed to the "Italian Church" of St. Mary's. Such were the early ethnic divisions even in religion. (Photograph courtesy of St. Ann's Church.)

St. Ann's today, looking exactly as it did in 1915. St. Ann's is one of the few churches that has enjoyed preservation without demolition. Intact, its choir loft is again in use, and it is resonant with the atmosphere of an old village church.

St. Ann's Church in 1915. Beautiful, it looks more like an Italian country church, with its tiled roof and hat-like bell tower, than most churches done in the Italian style. Not far from the church is the Sprague Mansion. Where the steps of the church are located once stood the house and store of John Gordon. (Photograph courtesy of St. Ann's Church.)

St. Ann's Rectory in 1886. This house is still used and the rectory is largely intact, a model of preservation. (Photograph courtesy of St. Ann's Church.)

A large group of teaching nuns at St. Ann's School. These sisters were called the Sisters of Notre Dame de Namar. They arrived and stayed until the writing on the wall dictated the school could not survive. It closed in 1972. (Photograph courtesy of St. Ann's Church.)

The interior of St. Ann's Church, facing the choir loft, *c.* 1927. Years later, the organ found its way to the floor at the rear of the church. It has since been restored to a former musical glory in the loft. The interior of this lovely church remains intact to this day. (Photograph courtesy of St. Ann's Church.)

A former well-attended Protestant church. Now a mercantile center, this graceful building with its bell tower intact was once a Protestant church. It was eventually overwhelmed by the Catholicism of the Irish and Italian immigrants.

The St. Bartholomew School in Silver Lake. Notice the shrine to the left, to the Madonna Dei Lattani, the patron of many of the immigrants to Silver Lake. The parochial school is noted for its high standing in the academic community. (Photograph courtesy of Mr. and Mrs. Robert Kennedy.)

The class of 1960, 28 strong. The school was to grow in numbers as the decades passed. In the center is Reverend Mario Beri, Sister Mary Cecilia (the principal), and Reverend Joseph. (Photograph courtesy of Mr. and Mrs. Robert Kennedy.)

Five

A Great House

A drawing of the infamous Sprague Mansion, the greatest house in Knightsville, bar none. (Drawing by Clifford W. Thurber.)

The Sprague Mansion as it looks today. The right side of the house, the old section, was built in the 1700s. The newer addition, grand and imposing, was a nineteenth-century creation, built as the fortunes of the Spragues increased greatly. Today all of the mansion is open to the public except for the private rooms in which the caretakers live.

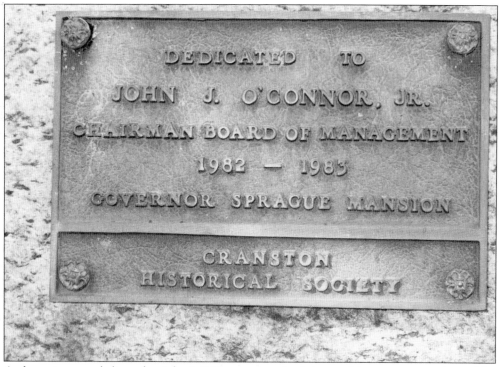

A plaque in stone dedicated to John J. O'Connor Jr., who led one of the great restorations of the mansion. The plaque is on the grounds of the mansion.

The entrance to the original house, on the right of the sprawling mansion. Built in the style of a typical eighteenth-century dwelling, only larger, it is very likely that Amasa Sprague came out of this doorway to meet his fate on his way to Thornton.

The imposing, dignified entrance to the three-story addition. This entrance leads into a superb hallway with a magnificent staircase.

The Sprague Mansion on a sunlit day. Recently, the mansion underwent a complete facelift that will take it nobly into the twenty-first century.

The dining area. Compact, comfortable, and elegant, it must be noted that most of the furnishings in the mansion are not original, for those were long ago sold off except for a few pieces. The furniture has come via the historical society and donations.

The living room. The original floors are still beautiful. Every attempt has been made in the restorations to reflect the two major styles of the mansion's history, even to the arrangement of the wallpaper in verticals.

A great room in the newer portion of the mansion. The grand piano is kept tuned and is used for various functions, parties, musicales, etc. This view shows the depth of the house from the front to back.

A view of the mansion from across the street. The tree in full bloom seems almost strategically placed in this photograph, which shows the division of architectural styles: the older part of the mansion (right) with its big chimney and the elegant newer part (left) with its cupola.

The stables. If you were rich, and you lived in a mansion, then to have your own stables was de rigeur. The restored building, once the victim of a fire, is at the edge of the sprawling lawn. This, too, is open to the public, a superb relic, much larger than most dwellings in the area.

Six

The Look of the Neighborhood

A nineteenth-century house on Plainfield Street. The area is rife with once-great houses, some of which have been restored, all of which remain stately. This house on Plainfield Street, not far from the St. Anthony Church, dates back to the nineteenth century. Notice the big chimneys at both ends of the house.

A large mansion on Laurel Hill Avenue. This beautiful building is now fully restored down to the trees on its spacious grounds. The big porch was an essential part of turn-of-the-century life.

A three-story house on Laurel Hill Avenue in Silver Lake. *More Stately Mansions*, the title of a posthumously-staged play by Eugene O'Neill, is a phrase that could also be used to describe many of the old, stately houses on Laurel Hill Avenue.

One of the greatest houses in Silver Lake. This unique dwelling, perhaps Silver Lake's most celebrated structure, has been meticulously restored by its owner. The elegant garage to the right is part of the property. It is really the showplace of Silver Lake.

Another very old mansion. Simpler, its lines more symmetrical and far easier on the eye, this very old house was a mansion in its day. Despite obvious additions (take a look at the air conditioner), this house in Knightsville still retains its quiet dignity.

A superbly restored mansion on Cranston Street in Knightsville. Now the offices of a chiropractor, this magnificent building is located a stone's throw from the two churches shown in this book. Essentially, the owner saved this building for posterity, and even with its very modern and essential alterations, it stands as an example of dedicated preservation.

An eighteenth-century dwelling, still preserved. This house in Knightsville speaks volumes of a time when the entire village was little more than a series of connected farms, dirt roads, and old cemeteries.

Another view of the stately house. If you look closely, you can see the white cross standing between the covered plaques against the white of the house.

Gemma's Bar in Silver Lake. If you want a drink in the Lake, if you have ever wanted a drink, chances are you have come here. This is a quintessential neighborhood pub, the "Cheers" of Silver Lake.

The Knightsville Pub, located "down the road a piece" (as New Englanders like to say). The Knightsville Pub is essential on Cranston Street. Much might disappear and the area will survive, but the survival of Knightsville is questionable without the Pub.

An absolutely unique six-sided house. There is no house like this in any other part of Knightsville and Silver Lake. Those are stone dogs guarding the gate.

Knightsville Post 14853. If a village does not have a veteran's post, then it does not really exist. Part bar, meeting hall, restaurant, and memorial, the Knightsville Post 14853 is a part of old Knightsville, and is still very active.

The Bathhouse in Silver Lake. No longer used for bathing, this is where the unwashed came for a Saturday night bath throughout the 1940s and even into the 1950s. The daily shower was a phenomenon of the future in village life.

The area where Silver Lake once was. When people speak of Silver Lake, whether they are aware of it or not, they are speaking of this parking lot! Dredged and gone, it is now the site of a shopping mall.

The waiting station for the busses on Plainfield Street. This building is so old, nobody can remember precisely when it was built. It has endured while contemporary versions in plastic and glass have disappeared. The trolleys stopped here, then the busses. Beyond is Neutokonkenut Hill, and across from the waiting station is the area where Silver Lake (the body of water, that is) once existed.

The old city hall. Founded in 1930, the building still stands in Knightsville, although the present city hall is a couple of miles away on Park Avenue.

The tenement houses of a narrow street in Silver Lake, looking much as they have always looked. These houses define street after street in the Lake. Silver Lake is also marked by hills. Nearly every street finds itself climbing to some point on Laurel Hill Avenue.

Row houses. Contrasted with the hills of Silver Lake and the tenement houses are these remarkably well-preserved houses of the "village," the row houses that served the mill workers. An equal number of houses are on the other side of the street; to the right is the great Sprague Mansion, and to the left is the Cranston Print Works.

The bandstand gazebo in Knightsville. This structure is the centerpiece of one of the annual festivals that takes place in the village. It represents one of more successful attempts to create a village green, a place where people of Knightsville may sit and talk and congregate.

A former church building. Take a long look at the car in the driveway, the envy of the world. This could be a photograph out of the early 1950s. It isn't.

The headquarters of the St. Mary Feast Society (Santa Maria Di Civita) in Knightsville. This building is a little bit of everything—a bar, a restaurant, and a meeting area (it even has a chapel, seen in another part of this book). The structure rising behind it is described in on the following page.

The magnificent Corinthian columns in front of the Knightsville Manor on Cranston Street. This colonnade is beautiful at any time of the year, especially when the vines are in full growth. People here wait for buses to downtown Providence.

The Knightsville Manor. Did ya ever think?? The high rise called the Knightsville Manor was originally controversial (it doesn't fit architecturally with anything in Knightsville). It now houses hundreds of elderly and challenged citizens.

The service station for city vehicles located in the middle of Knightsville. This garage, which services police cars and other city vehicles, has been located here for many years.

A house of cement blocks and (dare we say it?) vinyl! Authentic despite the intervention of vinyl siding on the upper floor, this apartment house on Cranston Street has a uniqueness all its own.

Vincenzo and Annina Abbaticola near a garden on Hillhurst Avenue in Silver Lake. Vincent and Annie always kept an abundant garden. The photograph is now 46 years old. Annie will be 101 in 1998. (Photograph courtesy of Josephine De Rotto.)

Seven

Where Generations Sleep

The "ancient" part of the sprawling St. Ann Cemetery in Knightsville, the burying place for 90 percent of the inhabitants of Silver Lake and Knightsville. This is the original cemetery, almost 200 years old. It dates from an era when the only immigrants were the English.

The family-owned monument business located close to St. Ann's Church. This business has carved and set thousands of stones in the cemetery. To its right is the Cranston Print Works.

One of the few remaining standing stones in the very old section of St. Ann Cemetery. John Dyer was a prominent religious leader, a deacon, and his family gave its name to Dyer Avenue.

A superb sculpture depicting the Agony in the Garden in St. Ann's Cemetery. The immigration of people from various countries in Europe can be studied here, for as one moves from an ancient burial ground of English settlers through the middle section of the Irish era, one finally comes to the front, to the ornate gates, an area where most of the names are Italian.

Another sculpture in St. Ann's Cemetery, this one created for the Ronci family by a Mexican sculptor. The theme of the Pieta is powerful and its depiction of agony and sorrow brilliantly cast in bronze.

The Pocasset Cemetery. Old, nostalgic, its hills and valleys are beautiful to walk. One of the most interesting cemeteries, it is as old as time, and contains a visual history in stone and slate of 300 years of settlement.

A monument to Private Clarence Surprise, a Marine killed during World War I in France. This monument to the young soldier was erected in the 1920s. His short life is still remembered with wreaths and a small flag on Memorial Day.

A dramatic closeup of the great bronze sculpture of the Ronci family burial ground. It is a strong, moving Pieta.

The river that flows under a bridge leading from Dyer Avenue to the Pocasset Cemetery. A beautiful spot, the river still evokes memories of a contemporary murder, and the search for a young man's dismembered body in its waters.

The familiar figures, the familiar pose: Santa Maria Di Civita protected in a glass shrine over a grave in St. Anne's Cemetery. The Cardi family is one of the best known in Knightsville.

A small temple, a mausoleum in the Pocasset Cemetery. Such above ground burial places were the prerogatives of the wealthy. This tomb is of stone and marble. Its floors are terrazzo, and its interior echoes the mausoleums of the wealthy of ancient Rome.

A contemporary version of an old theme. St. Ann's Cemetery to this date boasts three mausoleums, following the practice of the ancient Romans who buried their dead in the walls of great tombs. The cemetery has enough land for burials for the next 60 years or so, and mausoleums are becoming the burial place of the present and future, because of their compactness.

Eight

Feasts, Festivals, and Good Times

A procession through the streets of Silver Lake. The statue being carried is that of St. Bartholomew, patron of Silver Lake. Notice the houses that have not changed since they were built. (Photograph courtesy of St.Bartholomew Church.)

A blazing night scene at the feast, the carnival atmosphere favored by local churches for decades. Recently, St. Bartholomew has returned to a more intimate, family- and neighborhood-oriented feast, held close to the church. (Photograph courtesy of St. Bartholomew Church.)

The feast of St. Bartholomew. When the old St. Bartholomew Church existed (today only the bell tower remains as a memorial), the feast of the patron saint was a colossal affair, featuring parades and processions that sometimes lasted for hours. (Photograph courtesy of St.Bartholomew Church.)

The route of a procession. From street to street, past old houses and tenements, church societies and people march in honor of the saint. (Photograph courtesy of Mr. and Mrs. Robert Kennedy.)

The procession photographed in front of a three-story tenement. About the statue of St. Bartholomew are members of the Knights of Columbus. (Photograph courtesy of Mr. and Mrs. Robert Kennedy.)

A brass band passes GEM Ravioli, where homemade stuffed ravioli was created. (Photograph courtesy of Mr. and Mrs. Robert Kennedy.)

Pocasset Avenue in Silver Lake. Much has changed on this street, but what has not changed is the essence of the procession. Today, however, the procession traverses a much shorter route, and is more symbolic than all encompassing. (Photograph courtesy of Mr. and Mrs. Robert Kennedy.)

Another photograph of the procession moving through the streets. Little is left of what we are seeing here. The procession moves by businesses that have disappeared and houses that have been razed. Still, the row of tenement houses in the background remains standing. (Photograph courtesy of Mr. and Mrs. Robert Kennedy.)

The
neighborhood
tenement, still
an integral entity
in Silver Lake.
Street after street
is crowded with
closely built
tenements. These
houses have been
standing for over
70 years.

The seated statue of La Madonna Di
Civita. The statue is carried from St. Mary's
Church in one of the largest festivals in
the area. Knightsville has managed, despite
carnival atmosphere inroads, to keep its
festival very village oriented, close-knit,
and orchestrated by custom.

A swarm of worshippers and the beloved statue of La Madonna Di Civita. To the believers, touching the statue is tantamount to touching the living person. Mixed here is all the faith, devotion, color, custom, and superstition of the ages. (Photograph from the collection of Joe Fuoco.)

The shrine of St. Ann in St. Ann's Church on the feast of St. Ann's. No longer celebrated with pomp and carnivals and processions, this was once, however, a tradition in Knightsville.

The statue of St. Ann being carried from the church. More subdued than its neighboring church festivals, the emphasis here was one of family gatherings.

People outside near the church. Notice the proximity of the cemetery. Gravestones can be seen in the distance. (Photograph courtesy of St. Ann's Church.)

The St. Ann's Drum and Bugle Corps on the move. Behind them are the gates of cemetery named for their patron saint. (Photograph courtesy of St. Ann's Church.)

The Glee Club when it really sang. St. Ann's Church offered much to the young of the Knightsville parish, the glee club, the band, etc. But with the closing of the school, such organizations also folded. (Photograph courtesy of St. Ann's Church.)

A very honored occasion. Reverend Father Drury presents a National Civic Award from the CUA (the Catholic University of America). The sign on the wall that says "Down to the Sea in Ships" might be considered prophetic, when one considers the closing of the school. (Photograph courtesy of St. Ann's Church.)

Appreciation night at St. Ann's. On this night individuals of the parish were honored for their charity and devotion to the church. In this photograph, the woman to the left, Catherine Palmer (now deceased), was one of the very few female principals of a local school, May Westcott, in Cranston. Her sister, Jenny Palmer, was another. (Photograph courtesy of St. Ann's Church.)

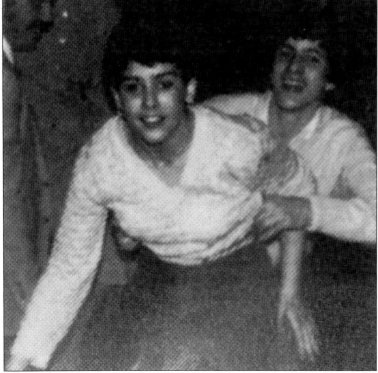

Playing hard to get . . . maybe. Patti McHale and Peter Antone enjoy themselves on appreciation night at St. Ann's. (Photograph courtesy of St. Ann's Church.)

A group of children at a feast picnic. At these picnics, the Knightsville parishioners from Silver Lake got properly rowdy. Are these children obeying or disobeying their leader? (Photograph courtesy of St. Ann's Church.)

The real way to enjoy a picnic. The seniors, as they might be too commonly called, sit it out, not running, jumping, or pulling on ropes. (Photograph courtesy of St. Ann's Church.)

An adult tug of war. Now to pull with some expertise requires that one be in great physical shape. "There are some that are, and there are some that ain't." (Photograph courtesy of St. Ann's Church.)

Frolicking kids at the picnic. Bear in mind that this was when the school existed, and its population was exploding. (Photograph courtesy of St. Ann's Church.)

A passion play at St. Bartholomew's. Big events such as this occurred frequently. (Photograph courtesy of St. Bartholomew Church.)

Three robust, cheerful kids of St. Ann's on First Holy Communion Day. From left to right are Doric Vieweg McKnight, Richard A. Vieweg, and Agnes Anderly. (Photograph courtesy of St. Ann's Church.)

A budding Dean Martin, or Jerry Vale. The older ladies seem unmoved—perhaps it's not their kind of music. (Photograph courtesy of St. Bartholomew Church.)

The Boy Scout troop of St. Bart's. These kids, chaperoned, are on their way to summer camp, giving their parents, as well as themselves, a break! (Photograph courtesy of St. Bartholomew Church.)

The 1957 version of the annual show. This show was put on 50 years into the history of St Bartholomew's Church (it has recently celebrated its 90th year). (Photograph courtesy of

St. Bartholomew Church.)

The Girl Scouts at St. Bartholomew's, in a photograph taken over 40 years ago. Notice the demure poses—certainly not out of the 1990s. (Photograph courtesy of St. Bartholomew Church.)

Pavlova, maybe, even Ulanova! She certainly has the look, the grace, and the prima-donna stance. This dancer was the Little Queen of St. Bartholomew's annual show. (Photograph courtesy of St. Bartholomew Church.)

The wedding day of Josephine Abbaticola. A well-known soprano, Josephine married Sam De Rotto and had two children, Joanne and Michael. To this day Josie and Sam live in "the Lake." Here she is pinning a carnation on her dad, Vincenzo, over 40 years ago. (Photograph courtesy of Mr. and Mrs. Sam De Rotto.)

Little Josephine and her brother, Vincent Abbaticola Jr. Not many were lucky enough to have a horse, especially one just big enough to ride. Note the size of the stirrups. (Photograph courtesy of Josephine De Rotto.)

A ritual of the ages. Who will get the garter? Probably the girl to the left of Josephine (Josie) Abbaticola on her wedding day. To the right, the very serious looking woman is Josephine's mother, Annina Zoglio Abbaticola. Today, Annina is 101 years old. (Photograph courtesy of Josephine De Rotto.)

The old staid-looking Knightsville Town Hall in 1905. the town hall was built in 1886. It was eventually demolished.

Nine

Parting Shots

A trolley moving none-too-swiftly along the tracks on Dyer Avenue. This trolley was a former horse car that carried passengers from as far, in those days, as Swan Point and Butler Avenue on the East Side of Providence to Dyer Avenue. (Photograph from the booklet *The Rhode Island Company*.)

Josephine De Rotto in an early twentieth-century costume, appropriately posing in an old garden in Silver Lake. Josie was a well-known soprano who sang widely in concerts and choral groups, inaugurations, and recitals. This photograph is now 50 years old.

Mary Abbaticola of Silver Lake in the 1940s. Notice how chic she is dressed, and how, ironically, one of the gentlemen in the window ad seems to be in the same pose. Mary., now in her 70s, was known for her superb penmanship, and was an Anthony Medal Winner in high school. (Photograph courtesy of Josephine De Rotto.)

112

Knightsville Corner on Scituate Avenue in 1910. These houses still are in existence. This photograph, taken in the late 1800s, shows the kind of construction that was popular during that time. The house in the middle is the Nathan Wescott House, and the roof of the Joy Homestead can be seen in the distance. This area was known as Joytown.

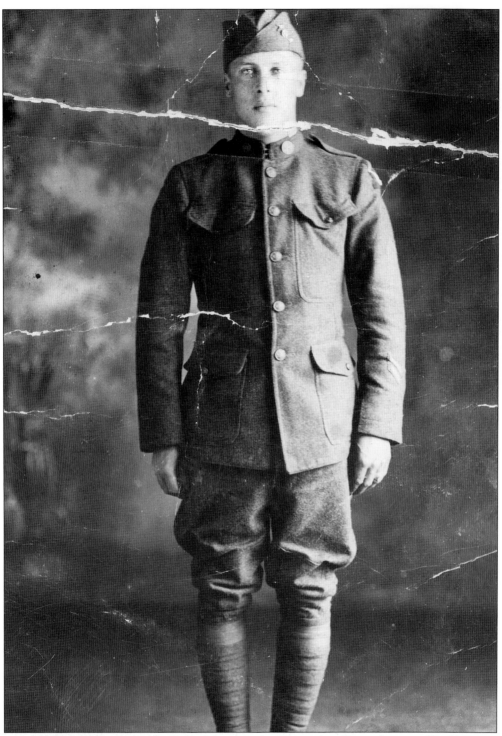

Mary's father, Vincenzo Abbaticola. Vincenzo lived into his 80s and was a World War I veteran. Handsome, with clear, sparkling eyes, he was known for his kindness and quiet. His wife, Annina, survives him. She is now 101. (Photograph courtesy of Josephine De Rotto.)

The Abbaticolas in Silver lake. From left to right are Josephine, her brother, Vincent Jr., and her dad, Vincenzo. It is Vincenzo in the World War I uniform, forty years earlier. This photograph dates from not long after the end of World War II. (Courtesy of Josephine De Rotto.)

Josephine De Rotto, the reigning soprano of Silver Lake. Here she is showing some show business pazazz on the stairs of a house in the Lake, 48 years ago. (Photograph courtesy of Josephine De Rotto.)

A photograph of Pasquale and Louise Grasso, who typify Silver Lake warmth and devotion. Louise has achieved some fame for herself via her cooking (she has made hundreds, perhaps thousands of pizzas for the St. Bartholomew Bingo nights) and her superb creations of altar coverings, pillows, and anything having to do with cloth. She is becoming one of the legends of the Lake.

Oresto Di Saia, famed architect. Di Saia designed many of the churches in the area, including the St. Bartholomew Church (the old church) and the basilica-like St. Rocco Church of Thornton.

Joseph A. Bevilaqua, who rose from extremely humble beginnings to become chief justice of the Rhode Island Supreme Court. Powerful, enigmatic, friendly, and controversial, he and his family for years dominated the politics of one of the most politically oriented villages in the state, Silver Lake.

John O. Pastore. Few men achieved such local and national fame as John O. Pastore, a governor and then U.S. senator. Still active today in his 90s, John was renowned for his oratory, his powerful way with words, and his drive. He is representative of a time in politics when the ability to speak persuasively and magnificently were essential talents. Today, it is a different ball game. (Photograph courtesy of St. Bartholomew Church.)

The Abbaticola family on a summer day in Silver Lake. The fence is not the proverbial New England white picket, but it is a picket fence, and obviously handmade. (Photograph courtesy of Josephine De Rotto.)

A man who brought more babies into this world than can be counted. When a baby was about to be delivered, Dr. Antonio G. Fidanza was there, often receiving for *his* labors a chicken, a dinner, something from the garden. Few doctors were as beloved as this man, Dr. Fidanza. (Photograph courtesy of St. Bartholomew Church)

The Giorgiannis, 50 years ago. The definition of an immigrant couple, the Giorgiannis, Antonio and Giuseppina, are shown here celebrating more than 50 years of marriage. Antonio survived his wife, but his devotion remained. (Photograph courtesy of St. Bartholomew's Church.)

Josie and Mary from the 1940s. These two little girls look so placid, a rainbow seems to have appeared above them. (Photograph courtesy of Josephine De Rotto.)

A group of conductors and drivers in front of the Dyer to Pocasset Cemetery trolley. In the far distance, the old houses remain to this day. You are looking toward Silver Lake. To the right may be seen the Rainbow Theater, a neighborhood movie house, now demolished. (Photograph from the booklet *The Rhode Island Company*.)

The Union Avenue trolley in 1936, making a stop on Laurel Hill Avenue, the street of mansions and beautiful homes. Walking in the snow are Antonetta Pullano (left) and Elizabeth Ronci.

A Christmas play at St. Ann's performed by schoolchildren. This is one of the charming memories of the school. Virtually the entire student body took part in the Christmas pageant. (Photograph courtesy of St. Ann's Church.)

The wedding of Annina Zoglio to Vincenzo Abbaticola nearly 80 years ago. Notice the opulence of dress and bouquets. It was also very fashionable for the boy ring bearer to be in a sailor uniform. Such customs did not belong only to the Russian Tsars. (Photograph courtesy of Josephine De Rotto.)

Annina as a teenager. An extraordinarily beautiful woman with a very pleasant personality, she is now one of the oldest, if not the oldest, residents of Silver Lake. (Photograph courtesy of the De Rotto and Abbaticola families.)

Three toughs (although they don't look so tough) on the sidewalk on Hillhurst Avenue in 1948. They were too young for the war that had ended a few years before, but they were prime for the war that was coming in a couple of years. (Photograph courtesy of Josephine De Rotto.)

Vincenzo Abbaticola. Considered, justifiably, one of the most handsome young men of his time, Vincenzo left his mark wherever he worked. A plasterer, he built thousands of walls in homes for people in the area and beyond. He was also a veteran of World War I and lived the remainder of his life on Hillhurst Avenue. (Photograph courtesy of Josephine De Rotto.)

Vincenzo on the stairs of a house he has been plastering. He lived well into his 80s. (Photograph courtesy of Josephine De Rotto.)

The wedding of Josephine Abbaticola to Sam De Rotto. To the right are Mr. and Mrs. De Rotto, and to the left are Vincenzo and Annina, Josi's parents. Annina is the lone survivor of the in-laws. (Photograph courtesy of Josephine De Rotto.)

Annina near her abundant garden. Her back yard seemed to be one magnificent garden, where all kinds of vegetables grew. She would sit outside on her spindle chair near her beloved garden, quietly smiling as always. (Photograph courtesy of Josephine De rotto.)

The family, la famiglia. This typical Silver Lake family consists of, from left to right, Sam De Rotto, Josie De Rotto, brother Vincent Abbaticola Jr., sister Mary, mother Annina, father Vincenzo, and the kids—little Michael and Joanne, now with children of their own. The event? Thanksgiving or Christmas. The place? The De Rotto home on Barrows Street in the Lake, a house famed for its open door policy. Everybody was welcome—everybody! (Photograph courtesy of Josephine De Rotto.)

A final parting shot, a treasured image. This is the great castle-crowned village of Itri, its tenement houses bringing a resonance of an old world way of life to a new world, a continuing echo not diminished by time. (Photograph courtesy of St. Mary Feast Society.)